£1.50

Allene Bowman Norris has spent all her working life in journalism. Even as a small child she won a book prize for essay writing in school. An avid reader, her career began in newspapers, magazines and then broadcasting and she spent over twenty years working as a reporter for BBC radio in the North-east of England. Before retirement she worked as a PR consultant and taught the subject to International students. She lists her hobbies as writing, water colour painting and enjoying the role of grandmother to her six grandchildren.

To Margaret,

GRANNIES LIKE US

Our finger-marks are together — with BT memories!

Allene Norris

Allene Bowman Norris

Grannies Like Us

Vanguard Press

VANGUARD PAPERBACK

© Copyright 2006
Allene Bowman Norris

The right of Allene Bowman Norris to be identified as author of
this work has been asserted by her in accordance with the
Copyright, Designs and Patents Act 1988

All Rights Reserved

No reproduction, copy or transmission of this publication
may be made without written permission.
No paragraph of this publication may be reproduced,
copied or transmitted save with the written permission of the
publisher, or in accordance with the provisions
of the Copyright Act 1956 (as amended).

Any person who does any unauthorised act in relation to
this publication may be liable to criminal
prosecution and civil claims for damage.

A CIP catalogue record for this title is
available from the British Library

ISBN 1 84386 281 6

*Vanguard Press is an imprint of
Pegasus Elliot MacKenzie Publishers Ltd.*
www.pegasuspublishers.com

First Published in 2006

**Vanguard Press
Sheraton House Castle Park
Cambridge England**

Printed & Bound in Great Britain

This book is dedicated to grandmothers old and new and to those who have yet to experience this delightful state. All the stories from the children are original. It depicts the joys and laughter and sometimes the worries of it all, and the way our role suddenly changes within the family.

GRANNIES' HELPFUL RULES, REGULATIONS AND TIPS...

Grannies	should be jolly and smile as much as possible.
Grannies	should be slightly overweight for all the hugs heading their way.
Grannies	should always be on call at a moment's notice.
Grannies	should count to ten before giving advice.
Grannies	should be able to keep secrets.
Grannies	should pretend at times to have lives of their own.
Grannies	should invest in good, strong flat walking shoes or heaven forbid …even trainers!
Grannies	should add to their shopping list, glucose tablets or energy giving drinks sportsmen use.
Grannies	should try to keep up-to-date with horrid fads and fashions even if they know their young relatives are likely to get pneumonia by wearing them.
Grannies	should suffer from impaired hearing from time to time.
Grannies	should immediately rush out and purchase a First Aid box, especially with Elastoplasts in it.

Grannies	should learn the difficult art of lip zipping.
Grannies	should always have huge bowls of fruit in the kitchen.
Grannies	should always be prepared to eat outside on a sunny day.
Grannies	should learn to swim if they don't already know how to do so.
Grannies	should try to master the computer to help with homework but plead they have no knowledge of such things.
Grannies	should build up a sweet and chocolate tin for special rewards.
Grannies	should invest in a sleeping bag. If it's not the child, the parents might be heading your way.
Grannies	should always buy loads of wet wipes, shampoo and bath bubbles.
Grannies	should aim to learn the skills taught in the diplomatic service.
Grannies	should learn that it is best never to take sides in a dispute.
Grannies	should be prepared to learn all about football or rugby or whatever is the favoured sport.
Grannies	should adopt the skills of story telling.
Grannies	should always relax their faces to giggle at anytime and be able to tell jokes.

Grannies should set out to discover where the best food is served in takeaways and cafes, which welcome children.

Grannies should always check out where there are clean public toilets for emergencies.

Grannies should always have the car filled up with petrol or have plenty of change ready for the bus.

Grannies should always remember on their first visit to a fast-food outlet not to ask where the cutlery is kept.

Grannies should never wear gear that is too trendy, being young at heart is the best thing and that is where it should end.

Grannies should be prepared to learn acting skills as the years go by:

FOR GRANNIES HAVE TO KNOW:

When to be shocked
When to be sympathetic
When to be intrigued
When to be astounded
When to be sad
When to be disappointed but not to show it
When to feel neglected but to remain cheerful

But the key skill – Grannies need to understand the parents but empathise with the grandchildren.

Grannies, as they get older should capitalise on the most valuable commodity that they have more of than any of their younger relatives, TIME. If spent with their grandchildren and used to great advantage, it is so rewarding.

Chapter 1

On Hearing the Great News

Mother Nature is very clever. As soon as we have got our children grown up and off our hands in a marriage or partnership, something else comes along for us to worry about even more ...grandchildren.

And the reason we fear for them more than we did for our own children is that it's all taken out of our hands.

"It's a boy" or "It's a girl." As soon as we hear those magic words announced by one of our children ...who is almost too choked with emotion to tell us the good news ...remember not only have THEIR lives changed, but we, the grandmothers can bet OUR lives have been changed forever. For gone are the mothers we once were, the organisers, the nurses and most of all the bosses. The people in charge are no more. But we wise grannies know this special day is the start of the most wonderful part of our lives. For it is true we suddenly have all the fun and not a lot of the hard work we used to have as parents. Hooray for disposables!

As soon as we see those tiny blue eyes gazing up at us (actually past us, for they can't focus yet) and see that first smile sent to a doting grandparent (actually wind, which we ought to remember as we have already had children ourselves) we are hooked.

Whoever wrote, "If I had known grandchildren were such fun, I'd have had them first," knew what they were talking about. For the grandchild/grandparent relationship can be one of the most intimate, caring and fulfilling bonds we can ever have. After all we are more relaxed than when we were parents. It is joy!

And notice how soon friends and family bring the new baby into the fold and give it an identity. "Doesn't he look like Uncle George?" (Uncle George by the way is 86).

"Eeeeh. He's got his father's nose, hasn't he?" and everyone hearing this is thinking we sincerely hope not. Thankfully, we grandparents just see the latest arrival as a totally new human being in a mainly wonderful world. Now isn't that rather special?

But before I get carried away…a warning. Grandchildren, we have to realise, like our children do fly and leave the family nest. We should be glad they do, for it is normal human behaviour and shows maturity on their part, and maturity on ours for accepting it. So those of us who understand this do not expect anything from our special relationship, just the satisfaction that we may have helped to give valuable guidance and been able to teach love and laughter to another human being during their formative years.

But back to that tiny bundle wrapped up in a shawl. The shawl could be a family heirloom, from a previous grandmother many moons ago, and would have been a garment hand-knitted or crocheted with the intention of it being handed down from one generation to the next. There must be very few grandmothers who carry out this fascinating task these days. Most of us modern-day grandmothers fill our lives with activities and events that would amuse our own grandmothers, if they could see us in action today. (I did try the knitted shawl routine, thinking it would be easier than the disastrous socks I had attempted some years before, but the finished product would never be wrapped round any respectable child and it ended up instead in the family dog basket where it was much appreciated!).

But there are two types of grandmothers. Those who are productive, making curtains for the baby's bedroom, knitting beautiful jumpers, sewing and spending hours making stylish clothes and bedcovers. This type certainly does end up teaching their grandchildren the most useful skills for later life, like cooking and baking.

My type sing songs, tell stories, entertains and keeps

children occupied and busy. I once thought this was the quite useless variety, but in fact it's not a bad thing to teach children to play games, to win and lose in life and to remain cheerful and optimistic, against all the odds. Of course, there are total geniuses, who combine both perfectly, but these are very rare grandmothers indeed.

But if you are just an average granny, like most of us, the best you can do is to offer to wash, iron, do some housework and baby-sit quite early on after the birth. We can remember clearly that the whole experience is a major minefield to the new parents who are terrified of this tiny little thing that has entered their lives, and has turned out to be much more of a responsibility than they had ever imagined. The easiest task for grandparents early on is pushing the pram, boldly and proudly, showing off the new addition to the family, to friends and neighbours. I always smile when I think how quickly that first magical birthday arrives (celebrated with such selfish gusto by parents and grandparents. Do you know a one-year-old who appreciated all the fuss and what was being done on that day?). But there is still a long way for the parents to go and lots to experience on the way.

Chapter 2

The First Baby-Sit

Grannies know instinctively that nothing is going to make us worry more than the very first time we are asked to baby-sit.

You all know the routine, we've had the experience of bringing up babies after all, and the thoughtful new parents have even left the restaurant's telephone number. Why then do we shake with anxiety and feel panic-stricken deep inside when we are asked to be in charge?

"Off you go and have a wonderful time," is the call to the couple that haven't dared to have a night out for weeks.

"The bottle is made up ready. Don't forget to boil the water thoroughly before reheating it. But don't get it too hot ..." The instructions from the diligent mother are still ringing out as the pair walk out of the front door, both looking anxious.

At this juncture grannies feel just as anxious, but don't show it.

"Enjoy yourselves, don't worry about a thing," is your second message to them both.

Why then, when the front door finally closes do we dash immediately to see if our grandchild is lying in the cot properly and is still breathing?

There's a special built-in ultra-protection system in grannies, which we all recognise, once we have been in this happy state and this is a time to put it into action. All is well …

So, you go downstairs and make a coffee, and are just settling into the chair, with the television turned on so low it is hardly audible, when there's a noise from upstairs.

It's only a murmur, and then a small gulp-like sound, then a choking that has you racing up the stairs nearly knocking your coffee over as you go. Panic stations!

By the time you have reached the top, great screams and sheer bellowing is going on in the bedroom, and once you get up there, you can hardly believe that one so small can actually make such a deafening noise. Grandad has wandered casually behind you, and is already infuriating you by being so laid back about the whole thing. (Secretly he's just as hysterical as you are). He comes out with "That child's hungry."

"Don't be ridiculous," you scream back at him. "The next feed isn't for two hours yet."

"Well, what are you going to do, then?"

How like a man to pass the buck, at this crucial time you can't help thinking. But at times like these grannies can easily ignore grandads and their unhelpful remarks.

"Come along my darling." Granny lifts the little one out of the cot, wraps the baby in a blanket and proceeds to carry her charge downstairs. It is a scary operation, taken gingerly. Each step one at a time, so aware of the precious bundle, and the actual descent takes five times longer than the ascent. Carefully. Lovingly in your arms.

This is what we excel at. Sometimes gently breaking the rules, but getting to the heart of the problem.

As soon as we sit down baby will repay us with a huge burp, from deep inside. Like its cry, you would never think one so small could have such a huge amount of wind inside such a tiny frame.

"There you are, I told you," says grandad, who firmly believes he does know all the answers in this situation.

We know instinctively what is needed. Baby facing our chest, peeping over our shoulder, and a gentle rubbing on the spinal cord. (If this were a cat, it would purr).

The gentleness of granny's hands, and the loving care bestowed on this tiny little human, eventually brings the one thing we want more than any other. Tiny eyes closed and baby asleep again. Granny tiptoes carefully up the stairs, and places the soft, warm baby back where it belongs, inside the cot. Not before she has checked all five fingers on each hand, and ten tiny toes. All is intact. Granny can tiptoe down again, to a cold coffee. (Who wanted one anyway?).

When an hour and a half later the same loud cries are heard once more, grandad turns as white as the baby towel in the bathroom when granny asks him to bring the screamer down, giving him instructions to be careful, while she prepares the bottle.

This baby is really yelling now, and grandad doesn't know where to put himself or the child. How on earth did he manage with our own children, you can't help wondering?

"There, there," we grannies whisper as we take the hot and bothered offspring and gently introduce the warmed up milk. Never is silence so welcome. The whole world seems to have stopped breathing as the little mouth sucks with satisfaction and pulls on the teat with remarkable force.

Both grandparents jump, and baby does too, when the telephone rings. But it's only the parents on their mobile phone checking that everything is all right. Grandad convinces them that it is, and returns to watching his wife looking soft and gentle with a face so kindly; the expression brings back memories of their courting days.

Shortly afterwards the doorbell suddenly rings, and the anxious-faced parents return early just as you knew they would, despite the reassurances earlier.

They always ask yet again, "Is everything all right?" and we always nod in a knowing way.

Little do the parents know, and thank goodness they don't, that we are terrified on that first occasion at the huge responsibility of it all as they themselves are, when they spend their first night alone away from the new baby. Wouldn't you agree?

Chapter 3

Learning With Toddlers

Those of us, who have experienced it, know there is a big difference between parenting and grand-parenting. The main one is that as parents you alone are in charge. In grand-parenting you are not. It is sometimes very difficult to keep your lips zipped when you see and hear things in relation to your son or daughter's offspring and their upbringing.

Grannies should be seen and not heard. Who wrote that? Well, I did. It is easier said than done, but worth remembering. It's a bit like when your child got its first bicycle. You knew there would be a lot of falling off, before it was mastered and you had to stand back and watch it happen. Grannying is like this, only more so.

Speaking candidly after you have been asked for an opinion can be somewhat unwise. Clever grannies learn to step carefully. It's not a good idea to go in with an 'I know it all from experience' routine to the new parents, for it nearly always backfires. You may not be saying what the parent really wants to hear.

If for instance, you see a huge Knickerbocker glory being served to the small child in the high chair, say nothing even if you think it will make them sick.

If you don't approve that the tiny tot is being bought a coat that costs twice as much as the one you are wearing, look away.

You might be shocked that the parents who have been saving all year are even considering taking your grandchild on a long haul holiday this year. When you know the baby can hardly appreciate the flight, scenery, cuisine or the heat, it's not for you to comment. So to tiptoe in with good advice, only if asked, is a better approach.

THE PLEASURES

"Granny, why is your face fraying at the edges?"

"Because I'm getting old."

"You're not old, you're new!" It tugs at your heartstrings.

Having this gorgeous little creature, who relies on you so much, is not only a pleasure but also a privilege.

Can you think of anything nicer than to go looking for crabs and sea shells on a lonely beach, an excuse for paddling in your tights, getting tickets for the pantomime, when you had wanted to go for years, but had no excuse to do so. (For what is a pantomime unless you can shout from the auditorium to the players on the stage?).

It is memorable to go gathering blackberries and making sure the small ones avoid the prickles too, or visiting a Pick Your Own strawberry field to collect fruit for the jam they love so much, if the fruit is not devoured before you get home.

It is now such fun to travel on trains, buses and look out of the window through the eyes of a child. Fleeting glimpses of animals in fields and those people waving back at you, often with small children themselves lifts your heart. And those unexpected autumn walks in the country looking for acorns and horse chestnuts take on a new magic.

Pushing that swing in the park until your arms ache, and feeling dizzy watching the roundabout's circular movement, surprisingly become pleasurable chores.

And as they get a little older and have pennies to spend, suddenly glitzy cheap and cheerful shops take on a new meaning, as the youngsters crave for some independence as they search for things to spend their money on.

And the patience and understanding you have to have!

If they choose to buy a book (which you always enthusiastically encourage them to do) it can take ages searching the shelves and then for no reason, they suddenly decide on a bar of chocolate instead! Another useful tip is investing in a few inexpensive things that will fill in many hours on those tortuous rainy days, when tiny legs in tiny wellingtons have had enough of splashing in the inevitable puddles. (RAINY DAYS AND HOW TO AMUSE - Another chapter) See Chapter 8.

Of course grannies are always aware of the dangers that surround us and for some reason toddlers are always fascinated by electricity wires, gas taps, and will even try pulling off the table cloth with the scalding teapot on it. In those early years it is a good idea to move the glass and favourite china ornaments a few feet up, to a shelf out of reach. Life is full of danger at this tender age and you can't take your eyes off them for a moment.

It is so exhausting grannies do admit, however guiltily, that it is often a delight and a relief when the refreshed parents come back to reclaim their overactive offspring. Now the grandparents, whatever their age or energy level can truly appreciate getting their feet up and watching television, perhaps for the first time that week.

Of course, we may not be the first to see their first tooth, experience their first step or hear their first word, but our hearts sing out whenever we hear of this progress. In fact if you beam and overreact to the child, I can guarantee he will repeat the word over and over again. Think how you would feel if someone who obviously doted on you was so easy to please.

Yes, being a granny at this stage, despite the high activity of toddlers, can be well recommended by all who have had this great exhausting and uplifting experience ...

Chapter 4

The things They Say…

"Did you die in the war grandad?" the four-year-old asked his rather startled relative.

***

"Auntie Vera, why do you wear pink lipstick that matches your nose?"

***

"Sorry I've been out of bed again grandad, but those squirrels outside my window were knocking their nuts together and I couldn't get to sleep."

***

In a letter to a northern grandmother who had not been able to visit south that Christmas:

"I hope you will be here next year, granny." So does she!

***

"You have to be careful when you walk near this river granny, for daddy says it is full of sultanas!" (She meant currents of course!).

***

"I thought you were dead!" a shocked grandson uttered to his elderly great grandfather who had identical looks to his late son, the boy's grandfather.

"Granny, was daddy at your wedding?" (Well, you never know these days!).

***

The nine-year-old boy was asked to answer questions about heaven at school. The teacher thought the easiest way of doing this exercise would be to make it simple. These are the written answers she got to her questions;

"What is heaven like?"

"Full of clouds and up in the sky."

"When you get there what will you see?"

"Flowers and bushes and nice houses and lots of toys."

"What does God look like?"

A pause, and then with conviction, "Alan Shearer."

***

On visiting with granny her new baby brother in hospital, Harriet says, "I think it's better to have a husband when you have a baby." Pleased with her moral stance, "And why is that?" granny asked.

"Well then you've got someone to take you to the hospital!"

***

"Grandad, can't you buy a car like this one?" pointing to a two-seater red sports car.

"Well I could, but won't because it is a selfish car."

"What does that mean?"

"If I bought one, I could only give grandma a lift in it, and you would have to walk."

A few days later:

"Grandma, grandma, there's one of those shellfish cars!"

***

"I'm really worried about this Aids." Sarah told her grandmother after a lecture at school. "Well don't you worry too much dear, for you'll get to know more about it when you get older."

"I'm not worried about myself granny. I'm not going to have sex. It's you and granddad I'm worried about!"

***

"How are your mummy and daddy at the moment?" Granddad asked little Mark who had arrived to spend the day with them. "They are very busy," was his reply. "Daddy is putting up a dildo rail in the dining-room."

***

Kathleen had accepted a sweet from a friendly man she had been chatting to on the bus. When they alighted granny commented, "You know dear, it's really not a good idea to take sweets from strange men."

"But granny, I don't know any men that are strange," was the five-year-olds swift reply.

***

"Granny, what a big bottom you've got," chuckled young Mark aged seven.

"Don't laugh too much, it runs in the family. You may have one this size when you're grown up," stopped his cheeky laughter.

PANTOMIMES …

I took my four-year-old grandaughter to see Cinderella at our local theatre. We left her two-year-old triplet sisters at home. I warned her that it would go dark, and then all the dancing and singing would begin.

Halfway through the second act, when she had sat there mesmerised, she reached up and whispered, "Granny why has

Cinderella only got two ugly sisters?"

***

The young man of about the same age had been warned that he would see a giant in the production of Jack and the Beanstalk. He kept turning round where two rows of empty seats were, then when they filled up with the bus load who had arrived late, he turned round in his seat and said to one of the ladies, "You can't sit there, that is where the giant is going to sit, when he comes."

***

Granny had got out of the shower, when her young grandson came into the bathroom. He was transfixed with the HRT patch on her arm.

"What is it?"

"A patch."

"Can I have one?"

"No, you can't. It is medicine."

"I have to take mine off a spoon."

***

The six-year-old boy decided he was sick of being nagged at when told to tidy his room.

"I'm leaving home," he told his parents. Mother looked startled, dad said, "OK off you go." They watched him pack a bag and walk out of the house. Four minutes later, after he had walked round the block, he was back ringing the doorbell.

"Yes?" dad asked.

"I've decided to give you another chance."

***

Grandad Bill was about to re-marry after his wife died. His four-year-old grandson went up to his wife-to-be in a room full of relatives who went silent after he declared in a loud whisper, "My Mummy doesn't like you. She thinks you are after Grandad Bill's money."

***

Young Elizabeth was reminded to thank Tessa for the chocolate Easter egg. (Remember her granny had always taught her to be honest as well as polite).

"Thank you Auntie Tessa, but I didn't like it. It made me sick."

***

Granny had told little Luke that grandad had died and gone to heaven. "I know, Mummy told me, but he hasn't arrived, for he hasn't sent a postcard yet."

***

"Granny, our school meals are really cool," Sarah told

her granny.

"Does that mean they are not hot enough?" the worried relative enquired.

***

The young granny of 58 years had just had her hair dyed blonde, mainly to hide the grey bits.

"You look just like Kylie the pop singer," the five-year-old told her.

Trying to hide her delight and appear modest she replied "I don't really think so!"

***

Always trying to educate, granny asked her young granddaughters who had just returned from Sunday school, if they knew who was the very first woman on earth. There was a long silence.

"I'll give you a clue. An apple."

"Granny Smith" was the immediate reply.

***

Young Cameron aged three, sobbed uncontrollably when he saw his grandparent's dog with a shaved back, clamps and stitches in, after an operation at the veterinary surgeon to remove a growth. His grandmother consoled him, but it was difficult, he was crying so much. Eventually on the way home from the dog hospital, through tears, the toddler asked, "Granny, can we call at the shop?"

"What for?" she asked.

Sob, sob, then, "To buy some fur for the dog!"

***

"We had sex talks at school today." Granny shuddered at the thought.

"What were they like?" she asked trying to show interest.

"They were all right, but I was shocked to think Auntie Sue had done that four times," was the reply that nearly had granny fainting, but she couldn't do so, she was laughing so much inwardly. And she knew her daughter Sue, mother of four children, would also smile too, when she heard about it.

***

Granny read Emily a bedtime story and when her eyes began to look sleepy granny stood up and said quietly, "Goodnight and God bless darling." Emily sat up with a start.

"That's not a nice thing to say," she told her startled grandmother.

"It's a lovely thing to say, Emily," granny assured her.

"No it isn't," Emily contradicted her. "When things go wrong in our house everyone says 'oh God' so I don't like you saying it to me."

***

Young teenager Sam was showing off the evening dress suit that his mother had hired for a formal music concert tour in France.

"Come and show your father how well you look in your first DJ. You look so smart I'm sure the girl musicians on the tour with you will be most impressed."

Dad looked at his son proudly and reiterated his wife's flattering remarks.

"Well if that's the case, and I look that good, don't expect me to come back with my virginity intact," the proud 14-year-old told his parents.

***

But this final story is about a child who remained silent.

Jack wondered why his nine-year-old son Simon was walking through the departmental store with his hands half covering his bowed face. Then he realised they were walking through rows and rows of ladies underwear. But it was not the knickers that made Simon blush and try to hide. There, just a few feet away was his grandmother and her sister frantically trying out the cut-price bras on top of their overcoats!

Chapter 5

Scary and Magical Moments

I once heard someone say that being a grandmother pulls at your heartstrings. Well, it is true. When you hear the little one has been rushed to hospital after falling off a swing in the park, you reach an all time low in your thoughts. And how your heart races. How careless of who was in charge to allow this to happen! Will the child still be alive by the time you get there? Did the ambulance come quickly enough?

Heartstrings …you're telling me!

You almost have a heart attack by the time you get to the hospital and have to be admitted yourself and then to your surprise and delight you see the little one, sitting up and smiling at the nurse, who is placing a bandage on their arm. All is OK this time …

The next event when you wonder whether your grandchildren will survive or not is school sports day. There is something about hearty P.E. teachers, that they always insist the event should go ahead whatever the weather. It is held on an open sports field, either at their school, or at someone else's and you can guarantee, even in the height of summer, there will be a harsh wind blowing, or it will be a day cautious weather men describe as having "squally showers." Your little dear is the favourite in the obstacle race and has begged you so you have agreed to be present. You are greeted by a youngster well schooled in charm (and with two front teeth missing) who hands you the programme.

At first you think the obstacle race has been cancelled. It is only when you are prepared to get your glasses out and read through the entire 88 events again, that you realise the obstacle race is the third from the last event. Even you, with limited sports and maths knowledge, can calculate that this must be at least two and a half hours away. But you are here now, and it would be churlish to merely return when your relative takes part, even if your hands and feet are already turning blue. The so-called thermal gloves and socks you bought from the winter Age Concern catalogue only last week, and you had thought would give you some protection, don't seem to be doing so.

Small children instinctively know how to scream like banshees for their house teams, and the only good news in this howling wind is that it does blow some of the very loud shouting away, and carries it down the field, thankfully in the opposite direction to your eardrums.

One hour fifty minutes later, when at last the obstacle race is looming, and you are practically frozen on the spot, as well as being mentally devoid of any feeling, you look in horror as the event is being set up. A ladder to climb, nets to crawl under, and the entire course looks exceedingly hazardous. The physical instruction teacher, who is wearing shorts and has a piercing whistle, blows it, and the eight tiny youngsters easily go through this maze before your very eyes. The one you are supporting is in the lead racing to the rope; you can't help but shout encouragement for the first time that afternoon. The voice they recognise as Granny's makes them turn towards you and give you a disarming smile thrilled that you are there and equally delighted that you are calling out for them to win. But as they turn, the other seven, streak past to the winning post, leaving your little one to trail in last. You still slap your chilblained hands together, and are only thankful that you can now leave this freezing place, and do not have to stand for another 60 minutes whilst all the semi finals and finals take place. Unless you are terribly sports minded this can be the most boring afternoon in the school calendar.

Grannies know that the heart will also beat rapidly at that other annual event that babies and toddlers do so well, the nursery school nativity play.

If parents are unable to be in the audience due to work commitments, grannies often have to be stand-in, and are delighted to do so.

As the curtain opens you are completely charmed by the tidy child with the golden curls that is playing the Angel Gabrielle and is now announcing "Behold, I bring you tidings of great joy!" And this isn't even your grandchild! It is such a joy to see the little ones performing, you coo over every child, and the more missed lines and stumbling over the words, the better! A tiny boy in his striped pyjamas walks on somewhat reluctantly, as one of the shepherds, and his mother whispers along the row that he is wearing one of her tea towels on his head, and quite fetching it looks too. Joseph and Mary hand in hand are approaching the inn and they make for the stable, where suddenly a star is pushed out from the wings and wobbles on its long stick. Joseph says in a stilted monotone, "Oh look Mary, a baby. It's what we have always wanted!" and a subdued titter goes round the audience. But when the chorus sings Away in a Manger, loudly and with conviction close to the cot, the audience can't contain its laughter when a small boy in the audience shouts out "What a quiet baby!"

Your youngster is one of the wise men, and you have not seen finer acting for a long time, you are thinking. The crown you made out of cardboard looks splendid and the old dressing gown covered in tinsel is shimmering perfectly under the stage lights. Just as you are beginning to think that this youngster may perhaps have a future in the noble acting profession, the crown comes off somewhat unceremoniously, and, a whisper to the wings "I've forgotten, what do I do now, Mrs Sanderson?" which brings more loud howls from the audience, and the young thespian in the dressing gown, insulted by the laughter, runs off in tears.

Of course they recover enough for all the carols, and collectively their sweet voices ring out reminding you about the true meaning of Christmas, and what a special occasion it is for children.

When we are lucky enough to be with our tiny grandchildren on Christmas morning, and we see the magic in their eyes, as they hold up a stocking filled with goodies, it brings back many memories of our own children at the same age, and of course our own childhood Christmases as well. And how tradition follows us in all families. As children we had stockings to open in my parent's bedroom, then we had to sit patiently and eat breakfast properly, before being allowed to see if there were any other presents in our front room. My son and my daughter carry out that same procedure in their homes, so I guess my grandchildren may do so in future years as well.

Chapter 6

Memory Making That Costs Very Little

Grannies should always seize the opportunity of building memories.

I have so many from my own grandmother and her beautiful stories about India, where she lived for a few years after marriage in the 1920s. Her sadness was that even as a young bride, she had failing eyesight and missed many opportunities of seeing the beauty of Bombay and the surrounding area.

But some remarkable things happened to her mainly because she couldn't see very well. One day she sat in the coolness of a tree on its own bough, and it was only when a servant came screaming to her not to move, that she realised she was in serious danger. A venomous snake had curled itself round the branch above her and was starting to slither down the main trunk. She had to choose the right moment to jump down and make her escape.

Another story she told was about the huge ant's nest she almost sat on at a picnic one day. She had not seen them either!

Her husband, my grandfather, was an engineer in India, employed to put electric lighting in Indian railways, and she travelled far with him on the overcrowded trains. She told us stories of much poverty and described to us how homesick she had been for her brothers and sisters in England.

When my grandfather came back on leave, he spent many hours alone, sitting in a canvas chair taking in the cool air of the Yorkshire moors amongst the bracken and the heather. All these stories were relayed to us as we sat at her knee.

Her childhood in Britain was so different to ours as well. In the cold, northern winters, when it was common for temperatures to drop dramatically, she often donned her ice-skates on the frozen river, which ran through the centre of her home town. She would glide under several bridges, in a long skirt, hands in a muff, en route to the local park. And because her parents lived close to the river, they had a boat and she spent many happy hours in the summer, rowing with her young friends, and ending up having picnics when they found a suitable riverside spot.

My sister and I, along with our male cousins sat enthralled and have never forgotten all the stories. The memory of them brings such lasting good thoughts, and best of all those magic moments of hearing them, cost nothing.

I'm not against cinema visits, but anyone can take children to the pictures, and however good the film is, the outing is soon forgotten. While tales to remember and special outings with grandmothers will always live on.

When I was young, going to the picture-house was indeed a special outing, for never had we seen anything like the glamour, dancing, the romance and the excitement that the silver screen brought us! And most grandmothers today will remember what excitement we all felt when tiny 12-inch black and white televisions came into our homes. Now, as our grandchildren consider it quite normal to see videos, have DVD access and 24 hour Disney channels, they find it hard to believe that when we were small we listened to the radio for all our entertainment.

That is why it is such a good idea to do something totally different and to put your grandmother's imagination into full throttle. Your own special days as a child will be re-lived too and you will build memories for the future.

OUR WEEK AT THE SEASIDE.

I remember my son asking if I could baby-sit for him to have a much needed break. I decided the best thing to do, as it was nearing the end of the summer holidays, was to take up the kind offer of a friend's cosy cottage on the Yorkshire coast in a fishing village called Staithes. It was a wonderfully simple holiday of walks along the beach, and when the tide was out, we walked on the rocks looking for fossils.

But it was memorable for other reasons, too. Shortly after arrival, we had to go into the nearest large town to buy warm trousers and more jumpers as it was so cold, despite being still officially summer. I even bought hand knitted hats from a local fisherman's wife, who was delighted to sell four in one go! It was too expensive to eat out every day, but when we did, we made it a really special occasion, and the girls thought it was wonderful to be a part of the fishing village scene that was so different to life in the town. They spoke to the retired fishermen too, who congregated in a sheltered spot on a bench overlooking the sea, where they put the world to rights. They told the girls they were members of the local choir and actually sang for us, so in return the girls practised for a couple of days and sang a couple of songs for their entertainment too.

One day it poured down from morning until night, so we didn't get far, but instead got the paintbrushes out and painted pictures indoors. A kind local artist had seen what we were doing previously outdoors, and had promised to judge their efforts at the end of the holiday.

I realised I was becoming very fit and healthy with all the clambering up and down in this tiny village that is a maze of narrow pathways and steps.

At the end of the day, we had a routine of the girls climbing into the steep, old enamel bath, two at a time, before going to bed. The fresh air and exercise soon knocked us all out and into the land of nod and I wasn't far behind the girls in getting into my own iron bed with its hard mattress.

But on the day we had stayed indoors, largely because of the bad weather, I had already made up my mind that we would do something different.

"Shall we get ready for the hot bath?" one of them asked at the due time.

"No, put your hats and coats on."

"Sorry?" They all gathered round looking at me in amazement.

"But it's dark outside, granny."

"Yes I know, but the rain has stopped and the strong winds have dried out the seat opposite overlooking the sea, and we are going to sit there with our cocoa tonight and watch the huge waves that are now coming in."

(You should have seen the scramble for coats, hats and scarves.)

And that's what we did! I took a tray with ginger biscuits and hot drinking chocolate, just across the road in front of the cottage and we all huddled together on the now dry wooden bench, sipping our hot drink and crunching biscuits. The noise of the waves was almost deafening which made it most thrilling, for them and for me. And what is most wonderful of all, it cost nothing, for what was to be a memorable experience.

DANCING IN THE RAIN.

Another warm summer night, as a storm approached, the children and I ran out into my garden in only bathing suits (and less in some cases!) in the pouring, warm rain. I can still remember those wet faces laughing, with hair plastered down, and those tiny feet covered in grass and daisies, tramping back into my kitchen, leaving a trail behind them, before getting into a hot bath. The mess (soon cleared up anyway) was worth it, just for another memory.

PAINTING PICTURES OUTDOORS.

One fine summer evening, we took all our paints and paper down to our local river, to paint outdoors. When we arrived at what I thought would be a suitable spot, we couldn't get near the river because of the huge weeds that had grown along its banks. We sat in a field surrounded by trees and close to the river instead and began to draw. About twenty minutes later, the gate behind us opened and a car came towards us. I thought it might be a farmer coming to give us a ticking off.

"I'm sorry, is this private land?" I asked.

"It's OK love. This is our fishing club's car park, stay where you are," explained the motorist who was now unloading his rods and bag.

My grandaughters still tease me for taking them to a car park to paint a picture. I remember the outing because they didn't want to leave even when the dusk began to fall; they had enjoyed the experience so much.

Grannies the world over will have similar stories to tell perhaps about even less expensive outings, and these are the memories that live on into adulthood.

Chapter 7

Words and Music

All grandparents learn very quickly that what small children love more than anything is being entertained in some way.

After all, by the time they have reached our homes they have had enough of schools, homework, and learning. But good entertainment can be an education in itself, if it is delivered in a subtle way. The children will not be aware of it, and this can be so beneficial in the end.

All good teachers will tell you that English and the command of it, is vital for every other subject. And it is such a vast and wonderful language, I get frustrated when I think that so little poetry is introduced in many of our schools.

But you have to tread carefully. Shakespeare, when introduced too soon, you can put a youngster off for life. The great Bard has to be discussed, and I think in its way, most poetry has to be as well.

So, when I thought my grandchildren had reached an age

when they would appreciate it, I bought a wonderful book called Classic Poems To Read Aloud, and the first poem I read to them was;

IT'S DARK IN HERE
By
Shel Silverstein

I'm writing these poems
From inside a lion.
And it's rather dark in here.
So please excuse the handwriting
Which may not be too clear.
But this afternoon by the lion's cage
I'm afraid I got too near.
And I'm writing these lines
From inside a lion
And it's rather dark in here.

I read this with great drama and feeling, but I was still astonished at their reaction.

"Read it again, granny," they cried in unison.

Then we discussed it, and talked about what it would be like to be inside a lion. They agreed you would be looking out past its teeth to the outside world, and one of them asked if the animal would have any fillings!

I was so excited at their reaction, I then read them The Lion and Albert by Marriott Edgar (one of my favourite comedy verses, which an uncle used to recite to me when I was young!) and I remember them later loving Matilda Who Told Lies and Was Burned to Death by Hilaire Belloc.

The King's Breakfast, by A.A. Milne was a favourite too, as well as I've Had This Shirt by Michael Rosen, the Owl and the Pussycat, by Edward Lear and an all time champion again by Michael Rose, Chocolate Cake. I'm sure there's not a child in the world who wouldn't love that one! They used to jostle to be the first to read it aloud themselves. What an exercise in English, pronunciation, presentation and understanding! We used to love our poetry sessions. Then, as they got older and we went back to being inside a lion, I asked them to write about something they could be inside or attached to, and stressed it would have to be something unusual. After all it would be quite out of the question to write something too commonplace! And they came back with all sorts of imaginative writing, inside a camera, and the flash went off too soon, trapped inside Dad's car and falling out when the horn sounded, perched on the school gate looking down at chalk and the blackboard. I never ceased to be surprised at what they came up with.

As they got older, I used to play them all sorts of music too.

"Shut your eyes and imagine what you can see." They then all wrote it down, and we discussed the very different ideas they had. All these exercises costing so very little, yet such fun for the grandparent as well as the children!

Chapter 8

Rainy Days and How to Amuse

ART

A little investment pays huge dividends on rainy days. For children of all ages like to be kept occupied, entertained or amused.

Some of the basics are: pencils, plain and coloured.

A selection of paintbrushes and paints. Water-based ones are the best, for they wash out of everything quite easily.

A big oilskin cloth for the kitchen table or lots and lots of newspapers.

Scissors, paper, lots of it, card and postcards.

Empty toilet roll centres, bottle tops, if you still get milk in bottles, old bits of wool, simple glue that washes out of clothes. Paste is often best.

Empty yoghurt cartons for water or paste. And empty egg boxes, (amazing what you can do with these, from Christmas bell decorations, to hats for dolls, etc. etc.).

Old beads for threading and making bracelets.

Old buttons, which can be used with dice to alternatively "give or take" from the person who plays the banker.

Collect shells from the beach and stick them artistically round an inexpensive mirror. Older relatives love these as presents and they look very good if they are painted, too.

Children will be amused for hours, if you can attract their attention with something unusual that they have never done before. The next two things amuse them more than anything I know.

Finger painting. Here we have to remember that there is no such thing as a total mess, just the wrong preparation in work-surface and clothing. For children to paint with their fingers you have to have the proper paint. It has to be water-based, and then it will wash out completely. Children are fascinated when you allow them and then teach them to paint with their fingers. It is surprising how creative they can become.

And another unusual activity. Baby-sticks, or baby-buds as they are sometimes called. These are quite cheap to buy and when crossed, stuck to the page with glue, or Sellotape will make lots of pictures. We used to paint the buds very bright colours. These look excellent as the centrepieces of flowers, and the children can paint the petals round them, and then add the stalks and the leaves. They love doing this on small cards, like postcards, and then they can be used later to send as greetings cards to friends and relatives.

VIDEOS

If your grandchildren do watch videos at your house, turn it into a learning experience. They'll love it if you make it competitive, so ask them questions about some of the things they have seen in the film, and offer prizes. This game will always help their observation powers and memories in the future.

I remember not being too well, when I had four small children in my care, and the only video I had that I thought might appeal to them was the musical My Fair Lady. They sat entranced through it all; though I thought, as it was fairly adult they would forget it just as quickly. They didn't forget it at all. Their teacher was highly amused when in the classroom, other children were singing "Postman Pat" and my grandchildren were singing "I Could Have Danced All Night."

Questions that followed were "Where were the men and women when everyone was dressed in black and white outfits?" (and by the way, the leading lady's expletive in this racing scene was so cockney my grandchildren didn't understand what she was saying, thank goodness!).

A simple, cheap way to entertain children, is to draw a six square grid on a large page and put into each one something for them to do. Sing a song. Dance in the corner. Draw an animal. Do a sum. Eat a sweet. Dry the pots. Your imagination can run riot on this one, and all they do is throw a dice. They love playing this game of chance.

BOARD GAMES AND CARDS

Play these by all means, for teaching them to win is so important, but learning to lose is even more important.

TALKING

Grandchildren should be taught very early on that grandparents can be told anything. It is particularly relevant these days, when so many problems can occur in families, and even if you know nothing about modern day entertainment, drinks and activities, always show an interest and let them know that they can talk to you about any subject. If we are prepared to listen, it is quite surprising what we adults can learn as well.

I decided to do some research so asked my six grandchildren, four leading questions. It was interesting to hear what they had to say ...

Your Earliest Memory?

One of them reminded me that I had turned my settee into a train, and then we had a Swiss roll cake at tea, dressed like a train with liquorice wheels, followed by The Railway Children video. (I had quite forgotten about this).

"And you always cried granny when the Dad came home" (which is true).

The other memories:

Painting pictures, out of doors whilst picnicking in the summer. The children coming down the stairs after a nap and drinking homemade lemonade. Using my staircase as an aeroplane and "flying" to a magical place. Making announcements, and serving refreshments on the stairs. Putting on a pantomime that neighbours and relatives came to see. All the proceeds went to charity.

What We Did?

Holidays and days out featured high on the list.

Baking simple cakes, icing them and then enjoying eating them.

One granddaughter reminded me of a holiday when we went shopping in a Spanish market, and bought fruit for the beach, and lots of clothes for her and her sisters. She also loved painting, but said the most important thing was being able to talk and discuss problems.

They reminded me that we once walked close to the

local river and collected stones from the bank that we brought home and painted. I loved doing that too. They make great paperweights and look good amongst plants in pots.

Are grandparents important?

Very. Yes, very. Someone to talk to and to laugh with. Yes, part of the family and they care about you. Yes, definitely. They are one step away from your parents.

One word to describe them:

Unique. Unpredictable in a jolly way, great fun. Spirited, larger than life, caring.

So it seems by this little survey, that laughter and being able to talk are just as important as being entertained. But I think most grandmothers would know this instinctively anyway.

Chapter 9

Grannies and Teenagers

If grannies feared for them when they were small (and we all did!) nothing on earth prepares us for the next phase of being a grandparent. We would be forgiven for bemoaning the fact that the years have gone by too quickly but we are near nervous breakdowns on seeing our sweet and innocent young grandchildren suddenly become ...teenagers.

Teenagers. The very word fills parents' thoughts with dread and for grannies a new era is dawning which brings lots of confusion, misunderstandings and a rush of blood to the head. Suddenly modern behaviour and so-called sophisticated education leave you thinking that you would really prefer to stay instead in your old-fashioned and even fuddy-duddy, comfortable world.

Those golden haired little darlings of yesteryear suddenly became tall, noisy, truculent, fashion conscious and independent but still manage to drag us their grannies, often unwillingly, into a world of pop music, cell phones, fashion and opinions that we can hardly believe exist.

Gone is some of the trust and simplicity you loved so much. The tiny, soft bodies that used to crawl into your bed sleepy and naked have now developed into the pubic state and lock the bathroom door when in the bath or squeal with horror if you enter when they are taking a shower. Suddenly size matters. The penis, the breasts, or lack of the latter create real concerns.

Now they hope we, the elders will support them blindly against what they consider to be strict rule-making parents. What they don't realise is that our hearts go out to our own children, the parents who seem to have a more and more difficult job to do these days than we ever did.

Here are three examples to make the point:

When we were young our parents worried about us coming in late (like 10pm).

When our children were teenagers we worried about them coming in late (like 11pm) and if they were drinking and smoking. Now, as grannies we worry along with parents, about our grandchildren coming in late (like 2am) and if they are drinking, smoking, having sex too soon or taking drugs. Does this list just grow and grow with every generation? Certainly the world has changed enormously and it is often hard for us to grasp it all. As pre-teen grandchildren we considered ourselves young at heart and "with it" (and don't laugh too much at that last comment - the teenagers will be doing it for us!) for indeed the expression "with it" is dinosaur language according to their calculations.

Chapter 10

One Liners That Fill Your Heart With Dread (compiled with the help of other grannies I know)

"It was a great party where everyone broke all the rules and had a fab time."

"I'll never have sex granny, for I hate boys and will always just have girlfriends."

"I can get my provisional driving licence next month."

"I've been looking at some bleach to go blonde."

"I might go on holiday with my friends this year, instead of boring Mum and Dad."

"Is it usual for periods to be late?"

"It'll be a great party on Saturday, for it doesn't end until two or three in the morning."

"Dad says I can't buy that see-through top, but I'm going to, as everyone has them."

"I want to get a perm and I want you to explain to Mum that boys do have them these days."

"I was thinking I might give up college and get a job to earn some money."

"I'm thinking of setting up house on my own for I'm sick of being nagged at home."

"I daren't tell Mum, so hope you will, for you can put it so much better, but I've lost the mobile she's just bought me."

Stepping out for the college concert "Are you really wearing that outfit granny? I don't think you realise how out of date it is."

"Mum says I can jump on a train, travel up alone and it will only take three and a half hours."

"My parents don't understand me granny so I might leave home and travel the world, finding jobs on the way."

"How do you know when you are in love?"

Miles away on the telephone "I have no money until tomorrow and have had nothing to eat today, but ah well, I suppose I'll lose some weight."

Chapter 11

Tales That Make You Smile ...some later

Trying to shock his grandmother, Sam told her he was going to Spain on holiday with his mates.

"What for?"

"For sex of course!"

"It seems a long way to go for that kind of thing. Can't you get it round here?" was the surprising reply that halted his verbal bravado.

***

Granny was proud to be asked to attend the awards ceremony at the college, where her grandson had won a major prize in sport. She dressed up for the occasion, wearing a new suit and smart hat. Arriving early to get a good view, she sat in the aisle seat at the end of the row, waiting for the event to begin. Her grandson had to walk in with other recipients in a line that moved slowly towards the platform. She looked up and smiled at him, as he passed by. She was totally ignored. When she asked later, why he hadn't seen her, he replied, "Sorry, but it was that hat granny. I couldn't let anyone know that a relative of mine would be dressed like that."

***

"I hope you've got your warm knickers on," granny called across the street to her grandaughter who was walking down with her schoolmates into town, one freezing morning.

***

My son took one of his four daughters to buy shoes that were suitable for school. "The ones he chose were terrible granny. No one would be seen dead in them," she told me later. The shoes the girl wanted were too trendy and had a heel that was obviously too high for school activities. Eventually they came to a compromise, by choosing something they both agreed upon, and about in the middle of the extremes.

"I've learnt one thing today dad," my grandaughter had stated. "You know absolutely nothing about fashion."

"And it will get worse, my dear," she was warned.

***

My friend was concerned when her daughter Lucy became passionate about a boy at her senior school. Her daughter was mooning about the house and spending most of her time texting the boy with messages full of love for him. Even when they went away on holiday she never stopped talking about the new love of her life, Michael. The parents were getting increasingly concerned for they hadn't met him. All they hoped was that their daughter was talking with such affection about someone they would like.

Weeks later, Lucy cooled towards him, but her mother had seen him waiting outside the school looking out for her daughter. He was wearing a bright orange luminous jacket and kept staring across at her and Lucy as they strode out to the car.

Two nights later the family had friends round, and the doorbell rang. Dad answered it and said, "There's a boy for our Lucy, what shall I do?" The front door was still open, so Mum whispered, "Has he a reflective on?"

"What?" asked dad. Mum repeated the question.

"I don't know," was perplexed dad's reply. "What shall I do then?"

"Give her a shout," mum replied. "She'll be playing her music so loudly upstairs, she wouldn't hear the bell."

Daughter was duly summoned and dad returned to the guests.

"What on earth did you ask me that for?" he enquired, obviously embarrassed.

"Ask what?" mum returned.

"If the boy had an erection on," was dad's answer to guffaws of laughter from their guests.

Later mum remarked, "What on earth made him think I would ask such a question? I'll never understand your dad."

But the comments were a family joke for years.

***

One granny I know was asking her grandchild what she wanted for Christmas.

"I'd like the Spice Girls latest book," was the reply.

And do you know what that grandmother bought? A spiced grills cookery book, which she had had great difficulty finding.

***

My friend took her two grandchildren on a bus. They ran to the back, as she was paying the driver at the front of the vehicle.

"Come back," she shouted to them. "We are getting off at the next stop."

"Why do you have one voice off the bus and a posher one on the bus?" one of the children asked in a loud voice.

***

Granny was shocked to find her early teenage grandson

had brought some pornographic magazines with him, when he had come to stay at her house. His older friend's brother had brought them back following a visit to Amsterdam. She decided to confront him about them, knowing that he had not intended anyone to see them, least of all his parents and that was why he had smuggled them to her house.

"Your grandfather will have a fit if he sees them," she told him.

Bright Mark, quick as a flash replied, "It was he who lent me them!"

So without his knowledge granny had a private word with grandad, who when he next saw the boy asked –

"Have you finished with those magazines I lent you, yet?"

The fifteen year old went as white as a sheet and said nothing.

***

My grandmother told me that they had to amuse themselves in simple ways when they were young. The highlight of my young life as a teenager was going on a bicycle, with a crowd of other young people down to the local river to take a picnic there. It was usually comprised of egg sandwiches and lemonade. I can remember smiling wryly, when my young daughter, in her late teens was picked up by a young man in his dad's sports car, and they took stainless steel wine glasses and a bottle of bubbly with them on their picnic. But one question I ask is, do young people even go on picnics with their boy or girl friends these days?

The same young woman came home from college ready for the summer holidays and announced that she was going camping with two other girls. Now a more unlikely candidate for the rough and ready experience of living in a tent I could hardly imagine. I advised against, but watched her pack high heels and smart dresses. She explained that these had to be taken in case they got any chances of going out at night. I had to contain my laughter (for she would have been truly angry with me) when she rang two days later, to say that she had moved into a nearby bed and breakfast accommodation, leaving her friends out in the fields under canvas. The word "camping" was never mentioned again in our house, until granny came to visit.

"How did your camping trip go?" she asked.

"Oh it was wonderful," was the surprising reply. "I found a really lovely B and B in the local village, and I'd certainly go on an outdoor trip in the country like that again."

***

Where did the old tearjerker songs go? My grandmother used to sing them to us, when we were in our early teens, and tears ran down our cheeks. One of them was about a young man who had a new suit of clothes bought for him, by his very poor family.

"But he died upon his birthday and never lived to wear them," were some of the tragic words. She also used to sing "No-one cares for me, not a friend in the entire world have I. None to calm my fears, none to dry my tears," ...etc. etc. and we always sat there with a lump in our throats and fighting back the tears. She was a wonderful drama queen!

***

Hannah had been particularly rude to her grandmother, answering her back on numerous occasions.

"Why is she so rude to me when my visits are so short?" granny asked her 9-year-old brother.

"Don't take it personally gran," he replied. "She is rude to me, sometimes cheeky to mum and dad who get very cross with her. Mum says it only happens once a month when she is suffering from DDT!"

***

Simon had obviously been taught nothing at home and had had everything done for him as a child. His rich parents owned acres and acres of land in Yorkshire and his parents employed two full-time servants at their lovely home. Not surprising then, when away at university he invited some of his fellow students round for a drink, he wasn't sure what to do, when one of them, Paul, stated that he didn't drink alcohol and refused the wine on offer.

"I'll just have tea," he told his host.

Simon duly went into the kitchen and did not return for ages so, one of the girls followed him in to see what on earth was taking so long. Simon had placed a porcelain teapot on a lit ring on the cooker. It was full of cold water, had a tea bag in it, and he was patiently waiting for it to boil!

***

"Quiet you'll wake my granny and although she doesn't mind me bringing some of my mates back overnight, I don't want her to come down. You'll meet her in the morning."

The three young men, who had been out with her grandson, tiptoed into the kitchen where they made a coffee and giggled and laughed as they had the inevitable inquest into the night out they had just experienced. Eventually, shattered they opened their sleeping bags and spread themselves out throughout the large house. The following morning the smell of bacon and eggs and coffee awoke them, and they gathered up their things and went down into the kitchen to meet their friend's elderly relative.

The look on their faces told it all.

They had all expected to meet a frail, elderly grey-haired

woman. Instead here was a woman full of energy, dressed in white tee shirt and shorts, before going off to her tennis lessons.

"Hi, boys, what would you like, full English?" she asked the speechless young men who were still suffering from the drinks and the late night …

***

One agony for parents when teenagers still live at home is where to draw the line in allowing them to "spread their wings," abide by the rules of the house yet give them some freedom about their dress-code and behaviour. Grannies should really stay out of this debate, unless in the "rag-trade" themselves, for teenage fashion will be something like their speech and use of slang …totally unrecognisable and unbelievable!

One very surprising development I saw with my own eyes was when two parents who I thought were quite strict, allowed their son and their daughter to attach chains from just about every part of their body. When I met them with their parents and tried to talk to the young people, I was mesmerised and couldn't take my eyes off the safety pins and other adornments cluttering their faces.

One day I met the girl with her grandmother. Her granny was a quiet, genteel sort of woman who I felt must be shocked at this statement her grandaughter was making, but to my surprise she remarked, "Quite a lot of metal to be carrying around eh? I wouldn't like to, but it's different and quite artistic isn't it?"

I wasn't sure how to reply.

***

Black was the thing. Black hair, dyed like a raven, black eye shadow, black lips and black nail varnish. Charlie was going through this "Gothic" stage and her parents and grandparents hoped she would soon grow out of it. All she would wear was black too and they all thought she looked like a witch rather than the pretty girl she was underneath it all. Granny was thrilled when she met her parents in town and was told that Charlotte had not only tidied up her room and thrown lots of things out, she was, as they spoke, decorating it.

"We don't care what kind of a mess she makes with the paint. The fact that she cares enough to do something to make it more respectable is good enough for us" they told her grandmother, whom they invited back for tea.

When they arrived back, Charlotte was washing her brushes in turpentine in the garage.

"It's fabulous," she told them.

"Self-praise is no recommendation;" one of granny's

favourite sayings from her youth.

"Go up and see it and judge for yourselves then."

The trio climbed the two flights of stairs until they came to the door with Charlotte on it. When the door was opened, they gasped in unison. Every wall was painted black and an antique chest of drawers had met the same fate. It took them quite a long time to get over the shock.

***

One parent told me that her mother was more than surprised when her grandson brought home a girl with a punk hairstyle and green painted toe and fingernails. Trying not to sound as if she was out of date or snobbish by commenting on the girl and the clothes she was wearing, the granny asked the young man who was staying at her home for the night, "I was surprised at the girl you brought in for coffee tonight. I somehow didn't think she was your type."

"You're right gran, she isn't. But it was a long way back to your house from the party and she was the only one who had borrowed her father's car."

***

As grannies get older and their brains don't function too well, they often suffer from a slowing down of the memory. Out of all the questions I asked at a youth club to research this book, the one thing that annoyed teenagers more than any other was when grandparents forgot their names ..."Fred, sorry Dennis, oh no, its Jack isn't it, save my legs and pass me that magazine I was reading, please." That sort of thing.

Chapter 12

Things That Teenagers Would Hate to Hear Granny Say……
(researched with a lively group of young people)

"I'm going to be daring this summer and get a tattoo on my bum."

"I'm getting rid of my car and buying a motorbike instead."

"We would never have been allowed to do that, when I was your age."

"I think I'll change my hairstyle and have it dyed pink with spikes."

"Your headmaster has asked me to sing at the school assembly tomorrow."

"I won't wait outside in the car when I come to pick you up from the college disco tomorrow. I'll come in and have a dance or two before I take you home."

In front of your grandson's girlfriend (about a

photograph):

"Isn't he a little darling lying naked on the sheepskin rug?" or

"Did you manage to get those two for the price of one - Y fronts in the sales?" or

"Guess who I sat next to at the party last night? Your tutor."

In front of grandaughter's boyfriend:

"I bought you that bigger bra that you wanted."

"I'm glad you brought Peter to visit me dear. I'll soon be able to tell if he is suitable for our family."

In a loud voice in a crowded restaurant "I don't care what people think. You are only seventeen once in your life, and I'm going to sing Happy Birthday to you, even if it does make you blush."

In front of friends:

"For goodness sake tuck your shirt in, it looks so scruffy hanging out."

Calling out "Bedtime dear, in you come."

Calling across the street on a cold day "I hope you've got your vest on." or

"When is your period due?" or

"Is this the friend who is not wearing a bra yet?" or

"Have you got your contraceptives with you?"

Chapter 13

Teen Speak

"I walked down the street with my wicked townie mate. He was telling me how mint the weekend had been. He was at a gig where he met a total beaua and she thought he was fine. Although she was a bogga and he was a twocka, they got on well. As we got towards school we passed the minging raggers in the yard, the geeks in the library and the nerds with their heads down. When we got to our pit, I shouted "Now then" as I entered the room. I got an after school which was shan. But the day rocked because in my detention there was a really fit dude so the day was ace after all.

Is that double Dutch to you? If you understand it, you are between the ages of 12 and 20 for it is true teenage speak.

A translation? Here we go then.

Minging …disgusting

Shan …sly or unfair

Mint …good, cool

Beaua …good looking

Townie …cap, tracksuit bottoms

Bogga …skate-boarder

Chav …(see townie)

Ding …stupid

Slapper …common girl

Fit …good looking

Fine …also good looking

After school …detention

Rocks …great

Now then …hello

Ace …the best

Twocka …common boy

Nerd …clever pupil usually wears glasses

Geek …clever, one who swots

Ragger …smelly and scruffy

Wicked …wonderful or great

Awesome …exceptional, memorable

That is the modern language in this 21st century. It makes simple teenage words we used like "smashing" and "fabulous," which were considered uncouth and slang at the time, very tame indeed.

Chapter 14

Love Is In The Air And Sex, Too

He loves me ...she loves me not ...She loves me ...he loves me not ... It's that time of the year again when Valentine's Day makes most teenagers suddenly long for romance.

Of course they don't admit it, and many poo poo the idea, but to get a Valentine makes their adrenaline pump faster and their hearts soar with satisfaction. Just watch any teenager, whatever their age, who doesn't get one, and you'll see what I mean.

One teacher friend told me that February 14th had become a major date in the school calendar; it mattered to teenagers so much. Even if they thought it might be a joke to receive one, they still liked to do so, as it proved somebody cared for them, even if only in a teasing way. And to produce one meant they didn't lose face in front of their chums.

Tony had decided to take a rugby book to college to be sold for charity. Although he still played the sport and enjoyed it immensely, this was a book he had grown out of, for it was bought a few years ago by his grandmother for one of his birthdays. The charity stall was filling up with all manner of things brought in by the young people who were determined to raise as much as they could for good causes. Imagine his amusement that evening, when his girlfriend called to his home with a present for him. All wrapped up beautifully, he opened up the book he had taken earlier in the day to the college charity sale. "I know you love the sport so much, I thought you would appreciate it. And can you believe it, it was bought for a Tony by his grandmother! Somebody else who bought it for someone they love," she told him.

"Well, well it was very kind of you," said the diplomatic teenager, who to this day has never told his now fiancé about the rugby book he still has in his bookshelves.

All of us, even we grannies know love hurts. But these days it also costs. And who foots the bill? The parents of course! How many text messages are sent every day with the telephone money that was meant for ringing home in an emergency?

And have you ever seen the telephone bill in a teenage house?

Some parents I know have put the telephone under lock and key, but here granny helps out and lets her grandson use hers. She might argue that it is not the cost that is so exasperating, but the fact that the line is always engaged and you can never get through. It is even worse when the line is connected to the house computer.

Nothing is more fearsome to teenagers than sex. They feel they have to talk about it to impress their peers. They certainly boast about it, even if they still remain virgins. And sex and teenagers is not only highly embarrassing to them ("Surely your age group doesn't do it, Granny. It's obscene"). But they create situations that go down in family history to be chuckled at forever.

One friend told me that at her all girls' boarding school, they had all called their genitals Lou. This was fine, until a pop star called LuLu appeared in Top of the Pops on television. The staff at the somewhat rigid school couldn't understand why in the free period, when they were allowed to watch this popular programme their pupils used to fall about shrieking with laughter in the only way that girls can.

I had an aunt that called her son's private part "his little pinky." Again television intervened …and it took some explaining to the now young teenager, why a programme called Pinky and Perky had suddenly become very appealing.

But my favourite story concerning sexual matters, was when a couple I knew who had five daughters, received a notice from school saying the head was concerned as the youngest one had been caught watching the boys urinating up a high wall. The parents agreed that the girls had been curious because they had not seen any male genitals, and it was really high time that they did. So, for the next few weeks, their father walked around their house naked. He left the bathroom, and wandered about in front of the girls making sure that they saw him without any clothes on. He said nothing, just walked near to them. They didn't even seem to take any notice. Then one evening when the family sat down to have supper of bangers and mash, the youngest who had been in trouble at school, pointed to the sausage in front of her and declared "Look everyone Daddy's bottom on my plate."

"That was bad enough," the father told me later, "but we were having chipolatas!"

Of course too early sex can have tragic results as we all know and the debate will go on forever about whether contraceptives should be available to very young adolescents.

Chapter 15

Putting The World Right

At some time during the growing up process, young people will attempt to put the world right. It is great that they do, and that they feel so strongly about local or world affairs, but we grannies have to hide a wry smile when they are talking about it passionately, for we have all been there before.

Some become vegetarians, others join political parties at their universities, others I suppose make bombs, believing they too can change the world by force instead of reasoning.

But to listen to a younger generation speaking with true feeling and conviction, makes you believe that perhaps the world is not such a bad place and there may be a future for humanity after all.

It is a great and admirable trait in the young, and parents and grandparents alike wish sometimes there was as much dedication and commitment to school and college studies. It is sad sometimes that youthful ideals are proved to be misguided at a later date.

Whilst some of my peers joined CND (the campaign for nuclear disarmament) and others went abroad as missionaries, I stayed at home and put my feelings down on paper.

I was very angry at one time when a titled person who lived in our area, got away with a serious motoring offence and I wrote these words at the time:

Your conduct has been really shocking
You've committed a terrible crime,
But seeing that Daddy's a JP
We're going to let you off this time.

You shouldn't have done such a dreadful thing
Your behaviour has made us all frown,
But considering Mummy's a former Mayoress
With a pardon we'll let you stand down.

We hope we haven't caused an infringement
On your social or business life,
Perhaps we should really pay you something
Pass on, our regards to the wife.

Chapter 16

How Things Have Changed

Anyone returning from Mars to this world today would be staggered at how all young people, who may look like individuals act exactly the same. Each and every teenager in the land seems to be walking along with a telephone to their head, listening or talking and holding the instrument in front of their chests whilst they stamp out text messages to their friends.

How on earth did we communicate with our pals?

We got on our bicycles and rode over to see them. We caught a bus and arrived to see our friends at their homes or we walked miles and miles to visit, that's how.

Teenagers today are forever worrying about their appearance. Spots, lip gloss, footgear are always high on the list of worries for girls and the boys are just as bad, having to have the latest designer shirts, football gear and hair styles.

And what did we have?

Boys "a short back and sides" hairstyle, all of them, which looked as if a pudding bowl had been upturned on their head and then the hair had been cut. And the girls? Longing to wear lipstick, but never being allowed to do so until our middle or late teens, as girls with red lips were considered "to be too fast for their own good." And shoes? It was only when we had left school and began earning a living that we were allowed to choose what footwear we liked. Of course there wasn't much choice either, but when I hear youngsters telling their parents what they want in shoe shops, I squirm. And these are school shoes the parents are buying!

And young people who progress and move on to colleges, always love to be treated like young adults, and one of the great events for them, is that they are allowed to shed school uniform so they can express their own personalities. And what do they do? Immediately all look alike, wearing jeans and similar tops with them. You could almost call their college clothing teenage uniforms. If you did, they would be very surprised.

And what were we allowed to wear?

Only school uniform, right up to the day we left. And the boys had to wear short trousers in the summer and long trousers in the winter however old they were. Some young men had to wear caps until they left school too. My husband once told me that for years after he left college and had been earning a living for several years, whenever he saw his old headmaster approaching him in town, he would jump to attention and immediately take his hands out of his pockets.

And make-up and hair changes: it seems strange to me that young women who have such lovely hair in their teens want to colour it. Time enough when the first grey hairs start to appear, that's what I say. And boys perming their hair!

What did we do?

We would have roared with laughter at any boy who set out to have a perm in our day. He would have been branded a cissy immediately and been the laughing stock in the community. Coloured socks were looked upon as daring. And girls? Our parents always accompanied us to the hairdressers, and watched over as hair was cut and washed. No one was allowed to decide on a new hairstyle until they had left school or college and gone out to work and earned the money that would pay for it.

For entertainment it seems teenagers have to spend money to enjoy themselves. Films, videos, meals out, visiting pubs, often under age, computers, DVDs, televisions in bedrooms, discos and clubs are high on the list.

And for us, at the same age?

Not much money, so occasionally film going, but mainly long walks and bicycle rides. But we were encouraged to learn to dance and occasionally went to dances in church or village halls, where we danced waltzes, fox trots, the Gay Gordons and the Ladies Excuse Me, which teenagers today would roar with laughter about, but laugh as they might, it was certainly one way to meet the opposite sex in a friendly sensible way.

I watched a teenager preparing a picnic, not so long ago, and smiled as I saw the effort that went into it. Her boyfriend was picking her up in his father's car, and she was preparing food fit for a king. Smoked salmon, tossed salad, cooked meats, fresh fruit and two goblets and a bottle of wine. Her friend and her boyfriend were going along too, so there was no risk of drinking and driving.

And our picnics?

First of all they were much more regular, as it was a cheap way to spend a day out somewhere. But we prepared egg sandwiches, perhaps an apple or two, bags of crisps and a bottle of lemonade. Then because we were on bicycles, it all had to fit into the saddle bag at the back. There were some squashed sandwiches on many of these trips, I can tell you, and often warm water in lemonade bottles. If we didn't go on our bicycles (and let's be fair the roads were much less busy than now) we used to catch a bus, or travel on the train to seaside or country.

I often smile when I think about the number of parties we had in our teens. Today young people have to go to pubs or clubs and stay out late to enjoy themselves. No party it seems is complete without spending money on alcohol, wherever it is.

And our parties? They were often held in each other's homes. It was a clever ploy, for parents certainly knew who we were seeing or going out with. Teenagers today would fall on the floor laughing if they were asked to play Postman's Knock (All the girls having numbers and the number called out meant you had to leave the room, and kiss the boy behind the door before he re-entered the room. Then the boys' numbers would be called when the "female postman" was out of the room). We all groaned inwardly if the door opened and it wasn't a boy we liked for his number hadn't come up!

The other game we loved as teenagers was Hyde Park Corner. A boy chose you as his partner. You sat on his knee, and the girl in the middle shone the torch, round and round the room. If she stopped it on you she took over sitting on the boy's knee, and you had to go into the middle of the darkened room and begin the procedure all over again. At least in this game, you got the chance to be with the boys you liked the look of. On a personal note, I went completely off this game, when I went to a friend's house, and her grown-up brother (he must have been at least 22 years of age) joined in, and when he pulled me down onto his knee and then kissed me, I tasted tobacco on someone else's lips and could smell beer on his breath for the first time, and although these things seemed terribly grownup, I absolutely hated it.

The idea of suggesting such party games to teenagers today is too much to contemplate, and how would they react if we suggested The Gay Gordons dance?

My friend told me that her 18 year old waltzed in the other day and told her that she had booked her holiday, which was a week in Lloret de Mar. My friend's heart sank as she could just imagine the hell of it. Noise, screaming, loud music, discos, clubs until the early hours and vomit and drugs.

"How much do you think I'll need to take with me, as spending money?" she had asked Granny, when Mum went out of the room.

"Don't ask me replied a startled Granny, who had no idea of teenage expenses.

"I thought about £150."

Mum back in the room now, "That won't be enough for all your food for seven days."

"Who'll be eating?" was the reply. "We'll just be drinking."

And food today? Young people are so used to quick instant meals, some of them have never tried the kind of foods we ate as children. Now, it is chips with everything it seems and frozen food is too readily transferred from the freezer to the microwave oven. Eating in the street has become popular and it is the instant hot sandwich or snack served from a polystyrene container and with a plastic fork. I feel sorry when I see teenagers eating like this as they walk along, and even sadder when the litter is dropped for someone else to pick up.

Our food? We had stews and soups, all homemade. Beef, pork or lamb and Yorkshire puddings on Sundays, and a joint big enough to make sure that there was enough to have cold on Monday (for Monday was traditionally wash day and mothers wanted something quick and easy to serve to us). If the rest of the week brought cheap cuts like flap of lamb or belly pork with all the trimmings you could guarantee that any left-over meat would be minced and used to make a shepherd's pie, with mashed potato and cheese on top. But Fridays were always fish days and if you liked fish it was a good day, if you didn't, tough. You had to get it down somehow, for there was nothing else on offer. It could be boiled, steamed, cooked in milk, but was rarely fried. That was the fish shop kind of fish, and you didn't have that too often. When we did, it might have been after a night at the cinema, and was a real treat. Eating it at about 11 pm. with piles of chips makes me wonder how we ever slept without having indigestion all night!

I never cease to be amazed at how young people take travel in their stride. By their teens most of them are sophisticated travellers who have been going abroad since they were small toddlers. I've heard from parents of children going on school trips to Tibet, Nepal, India, Canada, so France, Italy and Spain look quite tame to their well-travelled eye.

And us? I remember going to stay in a Youth Hostel with my school, about 40 miles from home. One girl cried several times during the week, she was so homesick.

Family holidays were about 70 miles, round trip from home, and were spent on the northeast coast of England. And how we loved them! Just living in someone else's house (no sleep-overs in our day) was a thrill, and we actually enjoyed swimming in the freezing North Sea. One beach is very like any other to a child, and looking for crabs, shells and even fossils, brought their own rewards. If we went to a café or restaurant, instead of returning to the cooked high tea provided by the landlady, it was a special day indeed.

We travelled by train to the resort (very few people had cars) which meant we had to walk everywhere. Most families did the same and were fitter and leaner than those of today. The ice cream tasted twice as good at the seaside for some reason, and after running backwards and forwards from our parents to the sea all day, fish and chips with the customary pot of tea and bread and butter, never tasted better.

Young people today seem to always have their heads

down studying, reading or writing, doing piles of homework and not daring to get behind in their college work. The types that don't take studying seriously hang about street corners and many do get into mischief, mainly on the drugs scene, as we all know.

I feel sorry for young people today. We appeared to have a much better balance of work and play. There seems to be little play now, unless parents really put themselves out to seek it. We played tennis at the local park, had roller skates, bicycles and seemed in general to make our own fun and entertainment. We hadn't enough money to make our fun expensive, but today our free activities would be considered too tame for the very little precious leisure time we allow our youngsters to have. What a pity the current system is so unyielding.

But despite all the changes, all the wonderful technology, all the shocks we grannies will get in behaviour and language for many years to come, most young people are remarkable, kind and caring. They deserve to have our unconditional love and support just as they have always had for generations before, and we should give it gladly as we watch the next generation of young adults finding their feet and facing an unknown future. What it is to be young? In an ideal world we should make sure that it is quite miraculous and beautiful and we should embrace it fully with our young charges and enjoy the privilege of being simply …a granny.

I hope you have enjoyed reading this book as much as I have enjoyed sharing my experiences and anecdotes with you. Do collect your own, as people have and shared them with us in this publication. They are as much fun as photographs as the family grow up and move out into the big wide world. But do write them down. We all think we will remember, but it is most difficult to do so as the years go by, and some gems disappear forever.

Here are two of my favourites from when the triplets were small.

My daughter-in-law used to dash to the supermarket once a week on her own to rush round and stock up with a week's groceries. Her mother looked after the three little babies and their sister at home, whilst she did this.

One day she was walking down the shopping aisle, when coming towards her, she saw another mother of triplets and friend of hers, who had her three in a buggy. The two Mums stopped to swap stories. They extolled the joy and the hell of having so many tiny babies to look after all at once.

As they talked, laughed and exchanged experiences, coming towards them was a small elderly lady. After selecting a can from the shelves, she turned round mouth open.

"Are they triplets?" When she heard they were, and after

admiring them all, she turned to my daughter-in-law and said "Now wouldn't you like three just like these, dear?"

And my daughter-in-law answered "Well actually …"

***

The triplets were very happy at nursery school and made many friends. One day, young Michael was asked by his mother, "It's your birthday on Friday. Who would you like to come to your party?"

Michael thought for a while and then replied "Danny, Simon, Mark, oh and the giblets!"

THE END

FOR ALL YOUR MEMORIES